*Equality, Status, and Power
in Thomas Jefferson's Virginia*

Thomas Jefferson by Benjamin Henry Latrobe.
Courtesy, Maryland Historical Society.

The Foundations of America

Equality, Status, and Power in Thomas Jefferson's Virginia

By J. R. Pole

The Colonial Williamsburg Foundation
Williamsburg, Virginia

Rights and Facts

When Thomas Jefferson of Virginia drafted the Declaration of Independence at Philadelphia in July 1776, he committed his country to a principle that became the centerpiece of its ideology: "We hold these truths to be self-evident, that all men are created equal, that they are endowed by their Creator with certain unalienable rights, that among these rights are life, liberty and the pursuit of happiness." He followed with the very important assertion that governments were instituted "to secure these rights."

Delegates from the South objected to and struck out Jefferson's further paragraph attacking the slave trade. But no one seems to have raised any objection to the theme of the Preamble just quoted. General agreement about the truth of these sentiments existed among delegations from as far north as New Hampshire and as far south as Georgia.

Yet anyone who looked around the plantations of Jefferson's Virginia or the other colonies would have known at once that even if all men were "created" equal, they certainly were not equals in the lives they lived or the opportunities that were open to them. It was also obvious that in the practical sense men were not equals in their natural endowments. It would have been much closer to the "self-evident" truth if he had declared that "all men are created different."

Jefferson, then thirty-three, had read much history, law, and philosophy; he was both sensitive and highly intelligent; and he did not need to be told that the men around him had unequal gifts, physiques, and abilities. What he meant must have had something to do with a *moral* endowment that remained constant in spite of these other—equally "self-evident"—differences. This highly prized equality, on which Virginians along with other Americans were ready to stake their lives, fortunes, and honor, was an equality of rights.

In their quarrel with the British authorities, the Americans for whom Jefferson served as such an eloquent spokesman had good reasons for being sensitive about rights. They were British subjects (the word "citizen" was not yet used)—subjects, that is, to the same crown. In that regard they claimed to be fully equal to other British subjects who lived at home in Britain.

During the mid-eighteenth century, however, they became deeply aggrieved to find themselves being treated *un-equally* by the British authorities. They were subjected to laws that did not apply in Britain and were taxed without their consent. For these reasons the leading colonists were acutely conscious of the importance of "equality" at the level of their collective political status. As British-Americans they felt themselves to be equal to the British in Britain, but they found that the British government did not treat them as equals. This distinction gradually alienated them and made them think of themselves, collectively, as Americans.

Within certain limits which we would not consider very satisfactory today, British constitutional law did treat all (adult male) subjects in the mother country as equals, but Britain did not apply its own legal standards equally over its American colonies. If it had, there would have been no need for Jefferson to reach out for the other source of rights in the Declaration of Independence—the laws of nature.

This was in some ways a dangerous doctrine to let loose, for the laws of nature—and "Nature's God"—were obviously superior to those made by men. If they held true, they must hold for everyone, everywhere. You could hardly have laws that were more natural for some than for others. The planters and gentry of the southern colonies had only to look into the faces of their slaves to see that when they appealed to a doctrine like this, they were raising questions which the doctrine could not answer. Yet they were not afraid to do so, and through the upheaval of revolution they maintained their places in a remarkably stable social order.

Those troubled years brought many changes in personal fortunes, in distribution of property, and in political power. But they brought no slave rebellion and no revolt of lower-class whites against their social and economic masters. The class that led Virginia into revolt against the crown was still substantially in power at the end of the struggle.

The emotions aroused by the doctrine of universal equality did have some very striking effects, to which we shall come later. But they have to be seen against a wider background. Virginia's great plantations and smaller farms, its little towns (Williamsburg had only some fifteen hundred inhabitants when Jefferson went to college there in 1760) and hamlets, its churches, markets, and courts were all scenes of occasional conflict, although the conflicting elements also knew how to live with each other. To understand the meaning of the demand for equality, its force, and its limitations, we have to set it in that much more complex society. We shall try to see how Virginians got to where they were in 1776, why they thought the way they did, and what consequences the Revolution brought to their society.

The Pattern of Patriarchy

When we consider the force and influence of the doctrine of equality by the time of the American Revolution, the first puzzle that confronts us is that men and women who had migrated to America did not come here with any idea of helping to build a more equal society than existed in Britain—or in whatever other country they came from. Those who crossed the Atlantic of their own free will did so with the aim of making better lives for themselves. Some were driven by the hope of riches; most of them probably thought they could gain some economic improvement and that at any rate things would not be any worse.

In eighteenth-century Virginia a "plantation" was what we now call a farm. Most of the planters worked to make a living from their own produce, which normally included some tobacco for the international market but also a fair amount of grain and other foodstuffs for the family's subsistence. The patterns of agricultural production changed, partly as the soil got "tired" of tobacco, but also as more and more planters— including the owners of greater estates—found that they could make better and safer livings from the export of grain and from raising livestock.

But whether we are talking about the great planters and slaveowners or the much lesser men, this matter of personal subsistence does give us a clue to the problem. The asset in their lives that they valued was not so much the possession or even the hope of great wealth. It was a certain measure of independence. A large number of individual farmers, raising enough to support their own families with some left over for the market, could feel securely independent of the lordly influence of their more wealthy neighbors. Most of them had very little notion of political philosophy. When we look at the way they and their families lived, we can see that economic independence, freedom to run their plantations according to their own judgments, and a sturdy sense of personal possession of their property amounted to the kind of equality that most of them wanted.

This was the sort of idea men had in mind when they asserted their right to equality (which they often did); they did not mean a society of equal wealth or possessions. Many of them were in fact tenants of the greater landlords. But if tenants needed the land, the landlords needed the tenants, and the rents did not reduce the tenants to poverty. Tenancy could be a step on the way to owning an independent freehold.

The value placed on equality was really an expression of the rugged personal pride of many thousands of individual and relatively independent farmers who wanted to be free to manage their own lives. But it was a value with very restricted application. Independent planters did not extend it to their servants, still less to their slaves. They also did not extend it to women, though that is a slightly different story.

An artist's portrayal of a southern plantation.
Courtesy, Metropolitan Museum of Art.

Differences between men and women involved the distribution of work and the authority for making decisions, but they were not differences of class. On the one hand, a servant or slave was a social inferior and was altogether likely to remain so. On the other hand, the small planter recognized that he was the social inferior of the great planter, but his independence came to the rescue to give him pride in his own self-sufficiency. Wives and daughters shared with servants and slaves the condition of dependence. Their personal status and sense of self, together with their economic subsistence, were subordinated to the male head of the family.

The prevailing pattern that dominated domestic relationships was thus one of patriarchy, which is defined as the authority of the father over his own family. It was generally assumed to be the natural order of family relationships, and it derived authority from much of the Bible.

How far did this idea extend beyond the bounds of the individual family—for example, between large planters who had great estates, a big stake in the international tobacco market, and numerous slaves, and their smaller neighbors who worked mainly for their own subsistence? We have given only a part of the answer to this question by explaining the importance of personal independence (which as we saw was almost a synonym for equality). The truth was that smaller planters accepted their place in a social order that in many respects seemed like a larger copy of the family pattern.

There were no genuine British nobles in Virginia. Titles of any sort were extremely rare except for those denoting military rank or ecclesiastical position and the designation of "esquire," a prerogative of councillors, barristers-at-law, some of the clergy, many county leaders, and some holders of public office.

Rank and title were important to those who enjoyed them, but it was not easy to insist on them among a crowd of independent farmers. Thus social life, though sometimes formal, could also be quite spontaneous. Life was often lonely, especially in the evenings, and men with big houses liked to entertain. In fact, one planter sometimes sent a slave to the local tavern to let the guests know that they would be welcome at his home.

When all this is said, however, the greater gentry did have some of the attributes of an aristocracy. Here is an account by William Byrd II, the second-generation master of one of the great tidewater estates, writing in 1726 of the mixture of greatness and responsibility that his position brought:

William Byrd II.

I have a large Family of my own, and my Doors are open to Every Body, yet I have no Bills to pay, and half-a-crown will rest undisturbed in my Pocket for many Moons together. Like one of the Patriarchs, I have my Flocks and my Herds, my Bond-men and Bond-women, and every Soart of trade amongst my own Servants, so that I live in a kind of Independence on every one but Providence. However this soart of Life is without expence, it is attended with a great deal of trouble. I must take care to keep all my people to their Duty, to set all the Springs in motion and to make every one draw his equal Share to carry the Machine forward.

In the last phrase, "draw his equal share" means "pull his fair share of the weight," and it is interesting, since we are discussing equality, to note that Byrd meant that every member of the community must do his best, not that they must all do exactly the same amount.

Byrd described the patriarch at home. The great families were interconnected, and there was another way in which they resembled and behaved like an aristocracy. An English clergyman, setting out for Virginia, was warned about it in these terms:

> John Randolph, [another head of a great family] in speaking of the disposition of the Virginians very freely cautioned us against disobliging any persons of note in the Colony . . . ; for says he, either by blood or marriage, we are almost all related, or so connected in our interests, that whoever of a stranger presumes to offend any one of us will infallibly find an enemy of the whole, nor, right or wrong, do we ever forsake him, till by one means or another, his ruin is accomplished.

Westover, the home of William Byrd II.

The great men also exercised a dominating influence (if they chose to do so) in the vestry, which was the body of parishioners who appointed the local minister and controlled the affairs of the church. The Reverend Mr. William Kay discovered this when he offended "One wealthy, Great, powerful Colonel named Landon Carter, a leading Man in my Vestry, whom I could not reasonably please or oblige." Kay had preached a sermon against pride that Carter took as a personal insult, so he got the vestry to turn Kay out of his post. Only after a long and bitter lawsuit, which passed from the General Court in Virginia to the Privy Council in England, did Kay win the case and receive damages. His friends had to find him a new parish, however.

The dominating influence of the great planters could also be seen in their houses. Their houses were not only larger than those of less wealthy men, they were also often situated in conspicuous positions from which they commanded the neighboring countryside. Their ground plans, with a large central block, wings at a lower elevation, and the kitchens, quarters for lesser fry, and finally the slave quarters set in visibly inferior relationships, all emphasized the sense of rank and hierarchy that held the social order together.

The laws reflected and reinforced this order. A servant did not have equal rights with his master. Nor did a wife with her husband. A servant who killed his master, a wife who killed her husband, or a child who killed his father was deemed guilty not just of murder but of the crime defined as *petit treason*. The point was that it struck not just at the individual victim but at the order of society.

Deference as a Social Force

The place of women in this social order probably did not differ very much from that in the older countries. It would be a mistake to think of women as nothing more than the victims of exploitation. On an ordinary farm, the wife and husband both had much to do to keep things running; there was a recognized division of duties, with the women, including daughters and female servants or slaves, feeding and looking after the animals,

Women were urged to "Keep Within Compass."

curing meat, churning butter, preparing food, and shouldering most of the domestic responsibilities. All this was vitally important. If it was in general lighter work, it was not less responsible than the man's labor in the fields. It was compatible with mutual respect, with frank discussions of such questions as what to plant next season, how much to put on the market, how to bring up the children.

But women were generally less well educated and frequently less literate than men. By the early eighteenth century over 60 percent of white men could read and write. We do not have figures for women, but they would be much lower. Women simply did not have access to as much information as their menfolk. During the Revolutionary War, when men were sometimes away for long periods, farm wives took more into their own hands, but they often had to seek the help and advice of male neighbors because they did not know the answers to problems that had always been left to their husbands.

On the larger plantations, the duties of wives were likely to be more social and less manual. They had to entertain, to plan the life of a larger household, to supervise a larger body of servants. (On the whole, upper-class Virginians preferred to think of their domestic staff as servants rather than slaves.) They also cared for the health of the community. A good deal of exhausting activity followed from all these responsibilities in the kitchen, the laundry, and the slave quarters. But they occupied positions of respect and their social and emotional rewards were no doubt often as comforting as those of their husbands or their sons.

What women could not expect to do was to break out of their fixed positions. They could not change roles, try a new profession, or go to town on their own to enjoy alternative entertainments. Men were much more likely to take advantage of and enjoy this sort of opportunity.

A male member of the gentry could be identified at a distance. His horse, his clothing and deportment, and the wig (or "periwig") he wore proclaimed his status. An elderly clergyman who had grown up as a poor boy in the 1730s once recalled the impression: "A *periwig*, in those days, was a distinguishing badge of *gentle folk*—and when I saw a man riding along the road, near our house, with a wig on, it would so alarm my fears . . . that, I dare say, I would run off, as for my life."

Manuals of conduct taught people how to handle themselves in the presence of their social superiors. Deference toward men of recognized superior rank had the effect of a cement to the social order; we shall see that it was questioned and even undermined by certain dissident elements shortly before the beginning of the Revolution (some people would say that such questioning *was* the beginning of the Revolution); but it remained as a great stabilizing force and had certainly not disappeared long after the Revolution, in the formal sense, had come to a close.

Some instances of deference helped to sustain the revolutionary cause by bestowing on Virginia leaders the same honors that were offered in colonial times to British dignitaries. When Peyton Randolph, speaker of the House of Burgesses, returned from the meeting of the second Continental Congress at Philadelphia in May 1775, he was met some distance out of town by the Williamsburg cavalry unit—"in order to meet our good and worthy speaker on his return from the continental congress," as a personal witness reported. Two miles from Williamsburg the company was joined by the city's foot soldiers, "who gave three cheers, and shewed every other mark of decency and respect."

A year or so later, just before Benjamin Harrison left for Philadelphia, a considerable number of people came to see him. According to the report of a visiting French nobleman (to whom Harrison told this story) they said: "You claim that our rights and privileges are threatened; we don't see how, but nevertheless, we believe you because you tell us so. We are about to take a dangerous step; but we trust you and will live up to your fullest expectations of us."

This basic trust and confidence in the superior abilities of the upper classes pervaded the courts and the elections to the legislature (which was called the House of Burgesses until the Revolution, when it was given its present name of House of Delegates). The county court conducted most of the business that affected people in their daily lives. The court was responsible for such matters as granting licenses to taverns, authorizing road and bridge maintenance, making local regulations, and hearing local complaints and grievances. Its members were almost invariably members of the upper gentry who were appointed by the governor on nomination from the existing members of the bench.

The House of Burgesses, which met in Williamsburg, stood at a greater distance than the courts from the people in their counties. Elections to the legislature did not happen very often—about once in three years as a rule through the colonial period. Elections gave ambitious men the opportunity to try out their standing with the public. The ordinary voters mixed in a familiar, informal way with the candidates, who often spent large sums of money on rum in the days before an election. This

The legislature of the Virginia colony met in the Capitol at Williamsburg.

kind of entertainment was known locally as "swilling the planters with bumbo."

From the conduct of these proceedings it would be easy to form the impression that a good measure of grass roots democracy existed, and in a sense this impression is correct. A large proportion of the adult white men qualified to vote by possession of twenty-five-acre freeholds with buildings on them, or twenty-one-year tenancies. A number of shorter-term tenants were sometimes permitted to vote by the sheriffs. So an election brought out a very good mix of the white self-supporting population as represented by heads of families. These men had a very real choice, and they often made their preferences felt. But they almost invariably chose members of the gentry to represent them. They would in fact not have wished to send to the provincial legislature anyone less than the most respectable, able, and preferably learned men among their own community.

This pattern of respect for power, reinforcing the holders of power, also took effect in the legislature itself. The House of Burgesses divided its work among several committees. An examination of the membership of those committees shows that they were always dominated by members of the leading families of Virginia. A new member of the House who was already distinguished by prominent social position or attainments received an important committee seat at once, and in any case would not have to wait long.

As population pushed out into the West, the British crown refused to allow new counties to be created with powers to send new representatives. As soon as the Virginians seized control of their own system of government in 1776, they created new counties in the areas where the population had already filled out. One result of this creation of new counties was an increase in the number of members who had little or no previous experience in legislative politics. Many of them were less well off than the average member from older counties and had less social standing. They supported some important social reforms, but in general it seems noteworthy that they tended to adopt the traditional attitude of deference to their seniors.

John Locke and Enlightenment Ideas of Equality

The leading members of society—those of the male sex, of course—had much the best of the limited educational opportunities available to Virginians. Some of them attended the small College of William and Mary in Williamsburg. Jefferson was educated there and was much influenced by his Scottish professor, William Small, who introduced him to some of the most advanced moral and political ideas of the time. Some large planters sent their sons to London's Inns of Court for training in law, others to the universities at Oxford and Cambridge.

After college, many of these better-educated men continued to read widely in the advanced thinking that was coming out of England, Scotland, and France. In this way they kept in close touch with the ideas known as the Enlightenment—to which, in their turn, they contributed in various ways.

We cannot speak of any single, dominant strand or character in the thought of the Enlightenment. Moreover, we must not make the mistake of thinking of the American colonists as if they were merely passive recipients of the writings of their European contemporaries. Americans made important contributions by their scientific observations of the natural world. By the very fact that government tended to be more relaxed in the colonies, that the churches were much less powerful, and ancient laws were less burdensome, Americans may be said to have unconsciously practiced some Enlightenment principles.

One important idea was that God must have intended to make his creatures happy and that governments ought therefore to try to help their peoples rather than to oppress them.

John Locke
by Sir Godfrey Kneller.

Another idea was that intellectual curiosity and scientific inquiry could help to solve human problems and ought to be encouraged.

English political ideas, particularly those drawn from the writings of John Locke (1632–1704), were influential in Virginia, where they encountered very little opposition or even alternative, and where they entered comfortably into a picture of the world that the planters could understand. According to Locke, society was based on a voluntary contract, made at some time in the past among adults who were already in possession of both property and an educated intelligence. Locke also said that at birth each individual's mind began as a sort of blank sheet (*tabula rasa* in Latin) on which experiences were gradually impressed.

Without going into the reasons for or against these ideas, it is not difficult to see that they contributed to ways of thought that were rather well disposed toward human equality. It seemed, according to Locke, that men's brains were equal at the start, and that inequalities were the results of differences of experience or treatment; it seemed also that the first contract must have been agreed to by men whose relationship to one another was as equals. There might be very good reasons for inequalities in the social order, but according to these ideas it was the *inequalities* that had to be explained and justified. It is important to note that Locke's system of thought did not lend support to the traditional belief that inequality was itself part of the natural order.

Locke's ideas were reinforced toward the middle of the eighteenth century by Scottish thinkers who emphasized a rational, benign, commonsense view of the world and taught that governments should try to justify their existence by making their peoples happy. Educated young men of Thomas Jefferson's generation were deeply impressed with these ways of thinking.

For these reasons, in spite of all the inequalities that kept men and women, masters and servants, white and blacks in certain very controlled relations with each other, men—especially educated men—did speak a political language that was friendly to ideas of equality. But one has to admit that it was more a language than a way of life. The inequalities that supported the economic system helped to pay for the education that made it possible for men to acquire and speak the language of equality.

Tobacco culture depended on slave labor.

Slavery: The Negation of Equality

Very much the greatest and most insurmountable of the inequalities was the institution of slavery. By 1750 Virginia had a total population of about 230,000, of whom 40 percent were blacks, and nearly all of the blacks were slaves. Slavery denied every possible principle of the Enlightenment, it denied human beings the freedom to develop their own talents, and it restricted their freedom to make their own moral or religious choices. African slavery had become firmly fixed in the Virginia economy only as recently as the late seventeenth century, but within a generation it took root with the growth of great estates as the dominant feature of plantation economy.

The men who lived from the labor of slaves often felt uneasy about it, especially after the 1750s and 1760s when certain Quakers and other religious persons began to question the idea of slavery on the basis of Christian beliefs. If it was morally wrong to wring a luxurious style of life from the toil of slaves, it also had bad social effects: it made men lazy and unwilling to set their hands to hard work.

But the masters could seldom see beyond the horizon of the world they knew. They could not imagine a world in which they would have to adapt to smaller farms worked by wage labor; they could not imagine a society in which whites and blacks might live as equals. They were trapped both by their economic interests and by their imaginative limitations.

One way in which educated men could rationalize the situation and explain to themselves that there was no reason to change slavery was to argue, from within their existing principles, that the slaves had never been parties to the original social contract. Consequently, they were not members of society; they were outside both its protection and its sphere of obligations. (Locke himself had said something like this, though he was manifestly uncomfortable about it.)

Another line of defense came from observing the existing differences between most whites and most blacks. It may be obvious enough to us that men and women brought from African tribal society, or brought up in America without the benefit of any form of education beyond the training they needed for work in the fields or workshops of their owners, would be unlikely to develop a wide variety of skills.

Africans and their children were visibly "behind" Euro-Americans in those things that the Euro-Americans did best. (Euro-Americans would have been just as far behind Africans in the skills that kept you alive and well in Africa, but these they did not need to have.) The many highly skilled black craftsmen could be regarded either as "exceptions" or as having reached the top of their attainments. So the whites came to think of the blacks as being "naturally" endowed with lower abilities, and they kept them in positions in which they would never be able to acquire higher skills.

This circle of reasoning worked well enough to save most white Virginians from inquiring any more deeply. But it is obvious, especially as they often encountered intelligent slaves, that they would not have been as easily satisfied if it had not been in the interests of their comfort and convenience to profit by slave labor and keep blacks at a marked social distance.

American slavery has had a long and bitter history which is not the central subject of this essay. On the other hand, we cannot discuss equality without coming to terms with slavery. Slavery provided the labor supply that supported the great plantations, and the great landowners in turn dominated the whole society.

Slavery by definition was racial slavery. It was impossible for a white person to be a slave for life. (Whites were often in effect forced laborers in the form of "indentured servants," but this condition lasted for a set term, usually four or seven years.)

The visible racial difference gave a great deal of added strength to the sense of social "distance," of an unbridgeable gulf, between white and black. This gulf helped whites to define blacks as slaves and then to convince themselves that blacks *ought* to be slaves—even that nature had intended it. The fact that blacks were slaves in turn reinforced the profound sense of difference and distance. This was a psychological barrier: in daily life, whites and blacks were often very much mixed up, especially on the smaller plantations where for some of the time they might actually be doing the same sorts of work.

Whites strengthened the system and contributed to making the gap more complete by the practice in law of defining the children of mixed sexual unions as black. The term usually used was "mulattoes." Law and custom ordained that mulattoes were classed as blacks. They took their status from the condition of the mother, and it was the mother who was more frequently the black partner. From the point of view of white masters this practice obviously worked very well. They got the benefit of additional slave labor from the mulattoes and they were spared the embarrassment of treating them as their own kith and kin.

Many thoughtful Virginians were worried about slavery. Jefferson wrote a pamphlet in 1774 stating the American case against Britain under the title *A Summary View of the Rights of British America,* in which he declared that the abolition of slavery was one of his "great objects." In his *Notes on the State of Virginia,* written in 1781, Jefferson included a plan for gradual abolition of domestic slavery. It is significant, however, that this scheme required the removal of the black population from Virginia, once freed. Neither Jefferson nor his contemporaries who disapproved of slavery on republican or humanitarian grounds could see a way around the race problem, as it appeared to them. (There is no evidence that this problem presented comparable difficulties to blacks.)

Such pleas gained so little support in the legislature or among the public that the Revolution itself cannot honestly be called an "opportunity" that was missed. There was sincere hatred of slavery among a few Quakers and anxious doubt among a few thinkers, but there was no antislavery movement. The most Virginians would do was to ameliorate the harshness of earlier laws for punishing crimes by slaves. The act of 1769 which did this explicitly said that these punishments were not in accordance with the dictates of humanity.

In 1772 the legislature made a major attempt to control the growth of the black population. It placed a heavy duty on slave imports and petitioned the crown to allow this legislation in the interest of closing down the African slave trade. The act was disallowed by the crown, which had no desire to see the slave trade ended.

Since this measure is sometimes regarded as evidence of antislavery sentiment, it may be well to explain the motives that lay behind it. Virginians had several reasons to worry about the rise of the black population: slaves were not inherently docile, their numbers could one day equal those of the whites, and newly imported slaves were the most likely to rebel. It also seems probable that the bigger slaveholders in the Tidewater felt that the value of their property might diminish with further imports. Considerations of humanity may well have been present, but they were rendered more acceptable by both fear and economics.

Early Challenges to the Old Order

Virginians were generally expected to be religious, and their religion was that of Protestant Christianity. Religious arrangements were in keeping with those of society as a whole. The Church of England was established by law. (The idea of separation of church and state had hardly yet been heard of; Jefferson and James Madison were among the first generation of Virginians to want to apply this Enlightenment idea to their own country.) All christenings, marriages, and burials had to be performed by clergymen of the church, and, nominally at least, everyone was supposed to attend services on Sundays or risk being fined. This requirement could not be enforced, but it certainly helped to confirm the official superiority of the Church of England over its rivals, the Baptists, Quakers, and Methodists.

Roman Catholics were officially disabled. They were not allowed to vote, had no political privileges, and attendance at Catholic services was subject to prosecution. The laws were silent on the subject of Jews or other minorities that were as yet either very small or nonexistent in Virginia.

The church in Virginia was very much a Virginia rather than an English church. Because England had never sent a bishop to the colonies, men wishing to enter the clergy had to go to England and receive ordination from the Bishop of London.

In the absence of a bishop (a state of affairs that most of the Virginia clergy could live with quite comfortably) the local vestries controlled parish affairs much more directly than in England. A minister had to please his congregation—or the great men in it, as the Reverend Mr. Kay found out. Since the vestry was responsible for the parson's salary, and the parson often had to struggle to lay hands on his pay (which usually took the form of marketable tobacco rather than money), the religious establishment was in many respects a series of local establishments. The "commissary" who represented the church in Williamsburg had much less power over the system than a bishop would have had.

Much of this account of Virginia society does not suggest very promising material for the growth of ideas of equality. We have noticed, however, some features that gave more opportunity for self-expression than usually existed in older countries, at least in the form of independence from social and economic overlords, and we have also noticed that many well-educated men were impressed by books that were sympathetic to such ideas. But the earliest stirrings of a distinct challenge to the supremacy of the master class came not from political radicals but from a dissident branch of the Protestant religion.

The first great challenge to the established churches of colonial America was the wave of religious revivals of the late 1730s and 1740s known as the Great Awakening. In areas farther north—notably New England—the established Congregational churches were riven with dissension; in Virginia, the established Church of England clergy felt threatened in much the same way. A Baptist church was founded in the northernmost part of the Shenandoah Valley in 1743 and "Regular" Baptists began to spread throughout the Valley. In the early 1760s people called "Separate" Baptists because they had begun simply by separating from the established church moved into the Southside, mainly from North Carolina. As their numbers grew and they settled throughout the Piedmont, they began to have unsettling effects that carried beyond religious doctrine.

Similar effects had already been provoked in the early 1750s by another Protestant sect, the Presbyterians. A brilliant, energetic young minister, the Reverend Samuel Davies, adopted the practice of itinerant preaching that disturbed the old order by its disregard for established "territory." Methodists entered

Samuel Davies.
Courtesy, Virginia State Library.

this scene only a little later and were picking up strength in the 1770s. The great Methodist itinerant, Francis Asbury, traveled thousands of miles in all seasons and weathers, not only to rouse the people from irreligion, but to counteract the teachings of rival sects.

By Asbury's time itinerancy had become more respectable. Its earlier effects were more socially disturbing, and in the hands of Baptists a new theology seemed to bear a new message about human society. The most important difference in the message itself was concerned with the content of religion.

The clergy of the official church were educated in theology and ancient languages, and they based their claim to interpret religion to their congregation on their knowledge of the biblical texts. There are many obscure passages in the Bible and much that depends on a knowledge of ancient history and languages. The clergy had the training to explain these matters, and they generally expounded the word of God as a matter of textual interpretation, or exegesis, as it is technically called. This

21

does not mean—as Baptists and other revivalists sometimes implied—that they were not sincerely religious, but it does mean that their standing in the community and their livelihood depended on public respect for their superior learning. Their learning entitled them to positions which in turn gave them considerable social prestige.

Learning and social standing meant nothing to the Baptists, especially the new itinerant preachers and their followers. They passionately believed that religious ideas that came only from books and religious belief that had to support itself by social standing cut right across the meaning of true religion. For them true religion came straight from the grace of God and was no respecter of persons—or, for that matter, of parsons.

They showed their differences from the old church in dramatic ways. For one thing they dressed in ordinary working clothes rather than in the gowns, buckled shoes, and even wigs affected by the established clergy. In this way the preachers made very clear the essential point that they, like their congregations, were ordinary people—that a person did not need to dress up to be at one with God—and that preachers did not need to distinguish themselves or distance themselves from the people. For another thing, their style of public speech was entirely different. They seem to have used far more gestures and more varied and intense intonation of voice. They addressed the audience in a direct way, including them in the action rather than just talking down and instructing them from a great height.

In the doctrinal sense, the way in which these preachers set egalitarian ideas in motion was to appeal to the religious witness of the individual's conscience. What this really meant was that everyone—man and woman, white and black, master and slave—had a conscience of his or her own, and that conscience had the last word in forming one's own religious convictions. This was quite different from leaving such matters to the opinions of an ordained minister of religion with a certain formal training and formal qualifications. It placed a great responsibility on the individual and it said that in this vital matter individuals were equal.

The Baptists also had a way of making this burden lighter and easier to bear, which they did by their strong sense of all of them being members of a religious community. They called each other "brothers" and "sisters" and, what is more remarkable, considering the general atmosphere in which they lived, they included blacks in this community. They encouraged and listened to black preachers. The strong emphasis they placed on sin and guilt may have caused their members a lot of psychological stress, but at least they regarded all men, women, and even children as sharing this burden of guilt equally. They did not believe that one could hold that before God some were more guilty, or more fallen, than others. So the emphasis of their preaching tended to make people think of each other as equals in a more positive sense than could be said for the Anglican church.

On the other hand, this tendency should not be taken too far. It did not free slaves. When the public authorities began to persecute the Baptists, some of them insisted that they were only teaching the slaves the Christian duty of obedience. Their primary concern was with salvation rather than emancipation. In the generations that followed the Revolution, they were increasingly careful to avoid appearing as critics of the institution of slavery.

The numbers of these revivalists were not very great, but they increased rapidly. By 1772 they may have amounted to some 10 percent of the whole population—about forty thousand by that date—and their concentration gave them political power in specific areas. (James Madison had to give weight to his Baptist constituents in Orange County.) As late as 1769 there were only seven Separate Baptist churches in all of Virginia, and of these only three were in the area north of the James River, which had the oldest settlements.

By late 1774, the number had risen remarkably to fifty-four Baptist churches, twenty-four of which were north of the James. These churches definitely appealed most strongly to the lower orders of whites, the humbler people whose birth and occupations placed them in dependent positions in society. They did not threaten that society with rebellion—on the contrary, their Christian purpose was peaceful. But their religious zeal did represent a moral renunciation of the social order that was upheld by the orthodox Church of England and its clergy. The Revolution, as we shall see, gave the Protestant sects an unprecedented opportunity to fulfill the claim to equality of religion.

From the spring of 1775, Virginians could foresee the threat of war; in July the Continental Congress called on a Virginian, George Washington, to lead the army. The way a people organizes for war always tells a great deal about its social structure. In the case of Virginia, the great men were more actively concerned with the apparent threat of British policy than of their social inferiors. British control of western lands, for example, affected the big land speculators like George Washington much more closely than it did the ordinary planters, and parliamentary taxation touched the pockets of the families who spent more on themselves for comforts and luxuries.

In Virginia as elsewhere, the leaders of society had to organize resistance through committees for making sure that the decrees of the Continental Congress were carried out in the counties. These committees tended to bring more local people into the procedures of government, even if only at a local level. One result was to strengthen the feeling of common men that they were needed by the country at large. If this feeling did not make them "equal" to their leaders, it brought them closer together and did much to fortify the self-respect of a wide population. In due course the broadening of the system of political representation brought more men of relatively humble background into the legislature itself.

At the level of military resistance, there were two different structures. One was the Continental Army, which had a thoroughly conventional system of military rank. Its officers felt themselves to be an elite corps with a special interest to preserve. In such ways, the very army that fought for American independence also put up obstacles to the development of feelings of social equality. It may be added that one of the greatest sources of friction was the intense regard for rank that men in uniform very quickly developed; no army fighting for equality of rights can ever have been composed of men more acutely conscious of the fine points of social distinction.

The other structure was the militia, raised in the counties, composed of local men, and officered by commanders elected by the troops. This was by tradition a much more democratic kind of military unit, and it brought men forward on their merits and their good standing with their neighbors. It remained true that the landlords were much more likely to be elected to the positions of command, for the same deference that suffused the electoral system worked on men's ideas about the proper order of authority for war.

Some years before the American Revolution broke out, a certain amount of discontent began to creep into popular feelings even about this "natural" leadership. In some ways the social leaders did not always set a very good example. Many of them were floating their high standard of living on debts that made their economic positions rather more shaky than must have appeared from their style of entertainment. Early in the 1760s many of the leading men borrowed from the treasurer of the colony, John Robinson, who was in a position to issue paper money notes that came in for withdrawal from circulation. When Robinson died in 1766, a rippling scandal began to break, threatening to swamp a large number of tidewater reputations.

We cannot say that on this and other issues the leadership was threatened with social revolt, only that there were visible signs of discontent. These manifested themselves in some of the elections that occurred in the early 1770s, when men with well-known names were occasionally turned out of their seats. So we are no longer observing a picture of uniform solidarity behind the leadership. This disunity got worse as the war dragged on for years without any obvious prospect of success. Small planters and laborers resented being hauled into military service for what some of them regarded as a war "brought on by the wantonness of the gentlemen, in which the poor are very little, if any interested."

It would also be a mistake to take the concept of "leadership" too literally. The leadership class did have certain interests in common, together with a sense of kinship, but its members were individuals, they did not all have the same interests, and they did not all hold the same opinions. These internal divisions were sometimes reflected in the legislature, where the revolutionary period brought some reforms—notably in religion—that had hardly even been contemplated earlier, and in other cases made it relatively easy to complete reforms that had already been coming through social custom.

From the point of view of equality, one of the most conspicuous of this latter class was the abolition of entail and primogeniture. Primogeniture was the old English rule that when a landowner died intestate (that is, without leaving a will) all the land passed to the eldest son. (Virginia law included slaves with land. When the legislature found that the law was not working in the interests of property owners and tried to repeal it, the crown disagreed. So the connection between land and slaves remained in force.) For many years historians wrote about the abolition of primogeniture as one of Jefferson's great reforms, and indeed Jefferson was rather pleased with himself for having convinced the committee on the revision of the laws that the eldest son deserved all the land only if he needed more to eat than his brothers. He regarded primogeniture as an unfair division of inheritance.

The real difference of opinion over the issue was more subtle, however. Jefferson wanted a society based on the individual; he was opposed, among others, by a distinguished lawyer, Edmund Pendleton, who wanted to retain a society built of distinguished families. Actually, it all made less difference than it seemed at the time—or than it seemed to later historians—because most planters did not die without having wills and also because there was enough land in Virginia to give opportunities to younger sons to become landowners even if the father's inheritance was not divided equally among them.

The old English practice of entail, a legal device by which the owner of the land was not free to sell off portions of it, was also intended to keep large estates together. It had long been used in a very relaxed way and without much restrictive effect in England, but Virginia had introduced a tighter system in 1705, a time when an emerging class of new landowners wanted to amass great estates and keep them intact. The rule did not work very well in their own interest because it caused difficulties for the planter who wanted to sell a portion of less profitable land in order to buy new land. Virginia was a superb colony for land speculators, but entail restricted the speculator's freedom and also made his estates less available as security for loans. Many entails had been "docked," that is, removed, by the legislature through private bills in the later colonial period.

Besides releasing lands for occupation by small farmers, the abolition of entail gave the greater landowners more flexibility in management. So this reform was helpful to all concerned. Virginia also passed a law by which a man's land could not be taken from him in payment of debts. This helped to preserve the property of small as well as large landowners and served as a measure of equality of property rights.

Independence and the Limits of Reform

Independence gave Virginia an opportunity to clear up the confusions, inconsistencies, and out-of-date aspects of its laws. The small committee mentioned above, whose main members were Edmund Pendleton, later a judge, George Wythe, a law professor, and Thomas Jefferson, attended to this business. For the most part, their work was that of clarification rather than setting out new principles. They restricted the death penalty to the crimes of murder and treason, but introduced castration as a punishment for rape. (Jefferson was afterwards shocked at himself for permitting this barbarity.) Since in general they let the old English common law rules stand, it cannot be said that the committee presented a program for carrying Virginia forward into an age of equality. And in the constitution of 1776, the rhetoric of equality was more emphatic than the political results.

The rhetoric is well worth attention, however. It represented the way men believed society had come into being, and therefore what they believed to be the basic principles on which it ought to be governed. If men formed society voluntarily, then nothing could justly deprive them or their successors of the conditions on which they had entered. Thus the Declaration of Rights (passed with the Virginia state constitution in 1776) stated:

1. That all men are by nature equally free and independent, and have certain inherent rights, of which, when they enter into a state of society, they cannot by any compact deprive or divest their posterity; namely the enjoyment of life and liberty, with the means of acquiring and possessing property, and pursuing and obtaining happiness and liberty.

This statement raised many of the same problems that were noted in connection with the Declaration of Independence. The Virginia legislature did not regard the Declaration of Rights as a mandate to convert the new state into a society of equals, even of equal white adult men. The legislature, however, did take certain important steps to make the legislative system itself more open to the people.

The right of suffrage was to remain "as at present," that is, a qualified voter had to own a one-hundred-acre freehold (with different qualifications for townsmen). Jefferson wanted to go much further and give the vote to owners of fifty acres while also offering fifty acres to every white man who would take possession and farm the land. Significantly, his colleagues thought this proposal too radical.

The new constitution also made no distinction between voters and representatives; anyone who could vote could be elected to the legislature. The qualifications were also the same for members of the newly constituted Senate. Even the governor could be an ordinary citizen. This principle differed from many other states, where care was taken to insure that only the wealthier citizens could fill the higher offices. It also helps to illustrate the fact that in Virginia the gentry felt rather secure in their positions of power.

Jefferson, who thought so much more thoroughly about social and political problems than most of his contemporaries, also developed a scheme for creating a statewide educational system. His idea was to establish three levels of schooling, starting with primary schools and rising to a state university. The students were to be selected for the different stages by competitive examinations. No doubt the system would have worked to the advantage of the children of better-off and better-educated families, but it would have given opportunities even to people with fewer advantages to enter a "career open to the talents."

The whole plan was defeated by the legislators' dislike of taxation. Most of them saw no need for an advanced educational system for the kind of work they expected Virginia's children to do. They had no inkling of the future need for higher levels of literacy and numeracy, and they did not want to encourage abstract ideas. If this imaginative scheme of Jefferson's had been put into operation, Virginia would have laid the foundations for a system of equality of opportunity.

Much later in his life, Jefferson did succeed in his efforts to found the University of Virginia. He rightly felt this accomplishment to be one of his great achievements and caused it to be commemorated on his tombstone.

Race and Law

It is tempting to think that a very clear line must have separated the old, colonial America from the new, independent Republic. Many of the political acts of the Revolution were truly revolutionary. Yet in Virginia—as in some other states—the closer we look, the harder it becomes to tell exactly where the old society came to an end and the new one began. The lines are blurred: many old habits persisted, and the basic order of society was not easily shaken. Where it had been shaken it tended to settle again on familiar lines. We must ask what differences the Revolution made, how much remained the same, and what things changed. To try to do this will help to place colonial Virginia in perspective as well as to understand

And to my mulatto man William (calling himself William Lee) I give immediate freedom; or if he should prefer it on account of the accidents which have befallen him and which have rendered him incapable of walking or of any active employment to remain in the situation he now is, it shall be optional in him to do so: In either case however, I allow him an annuity of thirty dollars during his natural life, which shall be independent of the victuals and cloaths he has been accustomed to receive . . . as a testimony of my sense of his attachment to me, and for his faithful services during the Revolutionary War.

George Washington freed William Lee in his will.
Fairfax, Va., County Circuit Court.

George Washington and his family. To the right is Washington's personal slave, William Lee.
Courtesy, Mellon Collection, National Gallery of Art.

what independence meant both to the revolutionary generation and to those who came after.

In 1798 a young Scottish traveler visiting Norfolk, Virginia, made this comment: "One half or more of the inhabitants are black, and slaves, moreover, in a country calling itself a free Republic. Out of ten thousand inhabitants five thousand are slaves who work for white people, who think it beneath them to stir themselves, and it is not at all uncommon for a white to keep blacks to let out as horses are in England." It is obvious that a generation after Independence, the great principles announced in the Declaration had not changed the basic labor system or the associated scale of human relations.

The Revolution itself was the only phase of this period in which the institution of slavery underwent any sort of ordeal. The British armies, if only for tactical reasons, offered liberty to runaways, and Virginia masters lost some thirty thousand slaves to the very people who were supposed to be oppressing Americans. The French army fighting alongside the Americans also offered shelter to runaway slaves, whose services they found useful.

Apart from these instances, however, the great majority of Virginia blacks remained relatively docile during the war—largely, no doubt, because they had little opportunity to do anything active about their condition. (The commonest form of slave "revolt" was for the individual to run away.) This good behavior, combined with some cases of actual black support for the American cause, convinced many Virginians that blacks deserved better treatment than they had received in the past. In 1782 the General Assembly passed a law permitting individual owners to manumit—that is, to set free—their slaves. Previously, every manumission had to be either an act of the governor and council or an act of the assembly.

It is clear that a number of masters took advantage of the opportunity to free their slaves. Some of them actually moved with their freed slaves to new settlements in the West. Others gave land to the freed slaves and set them up as farmers.

All this activity brought an increase in the numbers of free blacks and created for the first time a really distinct free black population as a marked element in society. In 1783 there were only 3,000 free blacks in the state; by 1790 the numbers had risen to 12,000—in a slave population of 292,000. By 1810 Virginia had a free black population of just over 30,000 and a slave population of 392,000. The free blacks were never very numerous, but they naturally tended to form communities where the whites used their superior power to hem them in. So, far from pursuing the idea of equality of opportunity, white lawmakers surrounded the free blacks with restrictions that kept them in a status of humiliation, subordination, and subjection not very far removed from slavery itself.

A series of laws passed in the 1790s and early 1800s tightened this subordination as the free black population grew. Free blacks had never been allowed to vote. Now they were bound to register every three years for certificates of freedom without which they were constantly at risk of being seized as slaves. In addition to ordinary property taxes, they had to pay a special tax, and if they failed to pay, they could be hired out for labor. Each black householder was allowed to own one weapon; otherwise, blacks were not permitted to share the whites' privilege of bearing arms. In 1801 an act of the assembly ordered that any free black moving into a county in which he was not registered could be arrested as a vagrant. After 1805, free blacks were not even allowed to organize their own schools.

The law prevented free blacks from receiving an education, except under white control (a rare occurrence); it prevented them from rising in the economic scale; it checked any aspirations among free blacks to feel themselves the moral or social equals of the whites who owned and ran the Republic. The law thus enacted a system that was much more oppressive than the class divisions of Britain because the very principle of equality before the law was denied, and the state made it extremely difficult for any free black to work his way up by his own efforts.

Free blacks became a separate and inferior community, living on the edges of the economy and constantly threatened as well as rejected by white society. They were denied equality in politics because they were bound by laws to which they did not—in fact could not—consent. In this way Virginia, like other southern states, consciously fostered not a class system but something more like a caste system where the whole life and expectations of the subject caste were determined by birth.

A black was normally considered to be a slave until he proved himself free. The law on capturing runaways denied the normal Anglo-American principle of a fair trial. Meanwhile, the liberty of masters to free their slaves was restricted.

White contempt for the black population was an old, ingrained habit of mind, constantly reinforced by the laws and customs that subjected blacks to degrading conditions. Because

RUN away from the subscriber in Albemarle, a Mulatto slave called Sandy, about 35 years of age, his stature is rather low, inclining to corpulence, and his complexion light; he is a shoemaker by trade, in which he uses his left hand principally, can do coarse carpenters work, and is something of a horse jockey; he is greatly addicted to drink, and when drunk is insolent and disorderly, in his conversation he swears much, and in his behaviour is artful and knavish. He took with him a white horse, much scarred with traces, of which it is expected he will endeavour to dispose; he also carried his shoemakers tools, and will probably endeavour to get employment that way. Whoever conveys the said slave to me, in Albemarle, shall have 40 s. reward, if taken up within the county, 4 l. if elsewhere within the colony, and 10 l. if in any other colony. from

THOMAS JEFFERSON.

Thomas Jefferson advertised for a runaway slave in the Virginia Gazette.

blacks were forced to do dirty work, whites could afford to live more easily and at the same time to enjoy the advantage of feeling superior. And yet despite this feeling, the whites were afraid. Their fears became much greater after the black uprising on the island of Santo Domingo in the early 1790s, which sent many French refugees in flight to the North American mainland.

Ever since Americans had begun to complain that George III and his government were reducing them to "slavery," they had been aware that their own laws deprived blacks of the very rights for which Americans were contending—rights they held to be theirs by the laws of nature. But it is hard to break out of a caste frame of mind—harder for the upper caste than the lower. One must remember that all the larger economic operations of Virginia depended on slavery; the great planters, including Jefferson, may have had moral doubts about slavery, but they could see no way of keeping their standard of living, their social display, their fine wines and carriages, even their own superiority in white society without slave labor. They soon came to fear that a large educated or prosperous free black community would begin to undermine slavery by its mere existence.

Some whites tried to convince themselves that blacks were in some way less than human and so failed to qualify for natural human rights. Others avoided philosophical reflections. Jefferson himself was extremely worried. In his *Notes on the State of Virginia*, he denounced slavery both for its inhumanity to blacks and for the moral damage it did to whites. He sensed that the system could not last forever and must end in a racial war, and he added ominously, "The Almighty has no attribute that can take side with us in such a contest."

However, as we have already noted, he could see no solution to the problem. Although his belief in relatively small freehold farms should have enabled him in principle to hope for an agriculture that did not need slave labor, he feared that large-scale emancipation would increase the danger of race violence. As he became more immersed in political problems, he set the problem of slavery aside for future generations to resolve. They duly paid the price.

Beginnings of Separation of Church and State

There were plenty of other problems, which from the point of view of whites in a white society seemed much more urgent than slavery. One in particular to which Jefferson brought his own strongest feelings was that of religious liberty.

We saw earlier that the Baptists mounted a challenge to the old order in the years before the Revolution. They objected strongly to having to pay for the support of the established colonial church, and later to that of the same church (now called Episcopal) when Virginia became a republic. They objected equally forcefully to the rules which gave that church official preeminence. The Baptists, in Virginia as in New England, were not committed by their religion to principles of absolute tolera-tion, but they were virtually committed to it by their position as a minority sect. It followed that they became advocates for religious equality, at least in the form of equality for all recognized religious sects of the Protestant faith (there was very little sympathy for Catholics).

The Baptists formed one branch of an alliance with Jeffer-son and his younger colleague James Madison. Jefferson and Madison, however, were cast in a very different frame of mind. They were passionately opposed to all forms of religious estab-lishment: there was no subject in public life about which Jeffer-son felt more strongly. He hated any kind of compulsion over the freedom of the individual's religious convictions and once remarked, "It does me no injury for my neighbor to say that there is no god, or twenty gods—it neither picks my pocket nor

*Patrick Henry
by Thomas Sully.*

breaks my leg." While Patrick Henry (who was becoming concerned about the decline of public morality in Virginia) wanted to give all Protestant sects official support, Jefferson and Madison looked toward something far more radical—the complete separation of church and state.

It would be quite wrong to think that this principle arose from atheism. Jefferson was deeply religious in the sense of believing that God had created all things, including the moral order of the world (which was part of the natural order). He did not believe in the divinity of Christ, but he seemed to believe in the moral values of Christianity. Madison was a former Princeton student of theology and perhaps had a more Christian disposition. Both men believed in liberty of conscience, a belief that sprang from a firm conviction that all consciences were equal. No man could therefore impose his beliefs upon others from his own sense of the evidence. Forced religious belief was not true religion at all—and it was in fact a form of blasphemy against God.

As a member of the legislature, Jefferson took on the most difficult contest of his career when he guided the bill to disestablish the Episcopal church. He succeeded mainly because the gentry were themselves divided.

Later, in 1784, with Jefferson away as American minister in France, Henry introduced a bill to incorporate the Episcopal church and to give equal establishment to other Protestant sects. Madison saw the danger and rallied the opposition. His own reasoning was expressed in a pamphlet called *The Memorial and Remonstrance,* in which he appealed very effectively to the principles of individual equality in Virginia's Declaration of Rights. He also warned voters that the same power that could establish all sects might later raise one above the others. There was safety only in disestablishing all sects, leaving them to find their own way, keeping the state's hands off the churches and the churches' hands off the state.

During this campaign Madison called up Jefferson's Bill for Religious Freedom (which had been sitting still for several years) and in 1786 successfully steered it through the legislature. In this way Virginia set the example that led soon afterward to the separation of church and state in the First Amendment to the Constitution of the United States. Once again James Madison, by then a member of the new House of Representatives, piloted the measure through the shoals of doubt and opposition in Congress and played a formative part in laying down permanent American principles of government.

We have seen that when Virginia leaders wanted to make the widest possible moral and political appeal, they called for equality. But they never defined equality very carefully—perhaps they were careful not to define it.

James Madison
by Gilbert Stuart.

35

At one level, equality meant that every adult white man could vote if he owned land, and in theory could be elected to public office. At another level, it meant that the laws were the same for everyone: there was no legally privileged class, there were no exemptions for the aristocracy or the church, and the law applied exactly the same way for everyone appearing for any reason in court. At the same time, the law formally excluded hundreds of thousands of slaves and tens of thousands of free blacks, who were relegated to permanently and irremediably inferior status, as though they were in reality inferior forms of life.

It is harder to be clear about the status of women. Like the rest of America, Virginia continued to be a man's world. Men not only made the laws, but they ran nearly all the plantations and businesses and were the heads of their own households. Obviously the women who shared those households had access to them and no doubt often exercised great personal influence. In some cases, women did manage their own businesses. At one time shortly before the Revolution one of the three newspapers in Williamsburg (all called the *Virginia Gazette*) was edited and published by a woman, Clementina Rind. White women could get a fair hearing in court, and they were treated with a respect that compensated (to some extent) for their inferior legal status.

The Revolution produced no dramatic transformation in the social or economic relations between the sexes, and the law left them unchanged. Yet everywhere in America the war itself was a social event that placed new duties and responsibilities on sectors of society unaccustomed to them. These sectors included women. With the men away either in the militia or the Continental Army, women often had to make decisions on their own—and some clearly relished their independence. They acquired a new self-confidence from the exhilarating experience of finding that they could manage people and property. In time they confronted their husbands with demands for a greater share in the decisions that affected the family's future.

This is not to say that women sought to assume masculine roles. For the most part, they shared with men a feeling that nature had ordained a distinction between the tasks allotted to the sexes. Women wanted more control in their own sphere, which generally remained domestic. We must remember that women were not able to organize. The agricultural nature of much of Virginia life even made it difficult for women to meet often or for long, except in formal family visits. Women were poorly educated. One consequence was that many of them failed to appreciate the benefits of education. There were exceptions, just as there were some highly educated upper-class women. In general, however, the war gave many women an opportunity to discover their deeper resources without offering them any change in the running of the political, religious, or economic life of their society.

Women's role was also reinforced by the war in a way that both raised their value in the community and at the same time fixed their duty as primarily that of being mothers. This outcome was not simply because an army needs men or that a new nation needs sons. It was because America was a *republic,* and a republic, it was generally agreed, needed virtue. Women came to be exalted as the exemplars and teachers of virtue. In subsequent generations many of them suffered from the psychological isolation and lack of human understanding forced on them by this role; it was a dubious benefit. By contrast with the prevalent colonial situation, however, there was a benefit to women when men were willing to recognize the true value of their contribution that gave them a higher status even in a world of men. It was not a benefit that could extend in any way to female slaves.

The Future: Opportunities and Contrasts

Where the idea of equality rested on the individual conscience, equality was very much the same idea as liberty. That was the thread that ran from the Declaration of Rights to Madison's arguments for religious freedom. In that respect, Virginia enacted into law the most egalitarian principles of the day.

After the new American Constitution had been launched in 1787 and a new government was in charge of American affairs, a new threat arose. This is not the place to examine the history of the Federalist administration. What we do need to note is that when Alexander Hamilton of New York was Secretary of the Treasury, Jefferson, Madison, George Mason, and John Taylor of Caroline County, among others, regarded his economic policy as a serious challenge to the kind of society they believed in. They were afraid that Hamilton's plans would create new forms of inequality based on money made from banking and commerce. They banded with like-minded men in other states (notably at first New York) to create the Jeffersonian Republican Party (the ancestor of the present Democratic Party).

The Jeffersonian Republican Party looked back to the principles of the Declaration of Independence. It wanted to keep in being the kind of agrarian society that had made the Declaration possible. It wanted, moreover, to keep opportunity open for men of small holdings to make their own way in the new world. To talk of this goal is to talk of equality on another level: equality of opportunity. No one used this expression yet, but the Jeffersonian Republicans were looking in that direction.

Virginia entered the Union and moved into a new era with a divided heritage. It is perhaps better described at the time as a robust society than as an equal one, but it did contain space enough for free individuals to feel their own strength and make—or lose—their own fortunes.

This sense of freedom and personal independence stood in for equality. In the Republic as before the Revolution, there was probably about as much equality, with the formal safeguards of equal access to the law, as most white men wanted for themselves. The avowed principles of the Declaration of Rights were more egalitarian than were the facts of life in Virginia. But the Declaration's rhetoric was a torch to light the way for new advances, and future reformers seized it as such from the hands of their forebears. Until then, pervading all, never far from men's and women's minds, was the presence of human slavery, human misery, and occasionally, among whites, inhuman fears.

Further Reading

Richard R. Beeman, *The Old Dominion and the New Nation, 1788-1801* (Lexington, Ky., 1972). Primarily about Virginians' attitudes toward federal issues, this book draws on much that is indigenous to Virginia thought and culture.

Daniel J. Boorstin, *The Lost World of Thomas Jefferson* (New York, 1948). Recaptures the world picture of Jefferson and his contemporaries, showing how much their ideas differed from those of our times as well as what we owe to them.

Jack P. Greene, ed., *The Diary of Landon Carter of Sabine Hall, 1752-1778*, 2 vols. (Charlottesville, Va., 1965). Carter was a great landowner and slaveowner. An autocrat and a man of science who prided himself on his knowledge of medicine, his diary gives extraordinary insight into upper-class life and much information about other social groups.

Rhys Isaac, *The Transformation of Virginia, 1740-1790* (Chapel Hill, N.C., 1982). An interesting study that uses some anthropological and non-conventional methods to get inside the different quarters of Virginia life in a period of crucial change.

Adrienne Koch, *Jefferson and Madison: The Great Collaboration* (New York, 1950). A study of the interplay of political thought and action.

Robert McColley, *Slavery and Jeffersonian Virginia* (Urbana, Ill., 1964). This was one of the earliest of the books that drew attention to the ways in which the Virginia social system and economy were based on slavery, whatever may have been the philosophical doubts of some thinkers such as—perhaps—Jefferson himself.

Drew McCoy, *The Elusive Republic: Political Economy in Jeffersonian Virginia* (Chapel Hill, N.C., 1980). An examination of republicanism in the context of political economy.

Donald H. Meyer, *The Democratic Enlightenment* (New York, 1976). There have been several recent studies of the Enlightenment in its American aspects. This is good on politics as well as such aspects as science and religion.

John Chester Miller, *The Wolf by the Ears: Thomas Jefferson and Slavery* (New York, 1977). Explains Jefferson's moral and intellectual dilemma.

Edmund S. Morgan, *American Slavery, American Freedom: The Ordeal of Colonial Virginia* (New York, 1975). Would America have been able to achieve its ideal of republican liberty if its colonial society had not been based on African slavery? This book raises and confronts this disturbing question.

William Peden, ed., *Thomas Jefferson's Notes on Virginia* (New York, 1954). Jefferson's only published book—against his own intentions. Both factual and reflective, this little work expresses Jefferson's opinions, doubts, and fears about his own "country."

Merrill D. Peterson, *Thomas Jefferson: A Profile* (New York, 1967). An accessible introduction by one of the most thoughtful and eloquent of modern Jeffersonian scholars.

J. R. Pole, "Slavery and Revolution: The Conscience of the Rich," in Pole, *Paths to the American Past* (New York, 1979). A discussion of the questions about slavery raised in Morgan, *American Slavery, American Freedom.*

Charles S. Sydnor, *Gentlemen Freeholders: Political Life in Washington's Virginia* (Chapel Hill, N.C., 1952), reissued as *American Revolutionaries in the Making: Political Practices in Washington's Virginia* (New York, 1965). The pride and personal ambitions of Virginia's ruling classes are brought to light as they struggle with one another, but not with their social inferiors, for power and influence in the institutions of the colony. An excellent introduction to social and political history.

J. R. Pole is Rhodes Professor of American History and Institutions at St. Catherine's College, Oxford University, England. His many publications include *Colonial British America: Essays in the New History of the Modern Early Era* (edited with Jack P. Greene, 1984), *Political Representation in England and the Origins of the American Republic* (1971), and *The Pursuit of Equality in American History* (1978).